MY
BIBLE
A B C's

Henry O. Adkins MPA

MY

BIBLE

A B C' s

Henry O. (HeNDRODIS)   Adkins

ISBN 0-9846083-5-4

by HeNDRODIS Adkins
(Henry O. Adkins. MPA)
first printing 1984
second printing 2011

My Bible ABC's

A ADAM

...ADAM was the first man.

1 Timothy 2:13

B BREAD

… Man shall not live by BREAD alone…

Matthew 4:4

C CHRIST

… for to you is born…CHRIST the Lord.

Luke 2:11

D DEVIL

Little children…
he who does
right is righteous…
He who commits
sin is of the DEVIL.

1John 3:7-8

E EYES

...Blessed are your EYES...

Matthew 13:16

F FATHER

…honor your FATHER and mother …

Ephesians 6:2
Matthew 15:4
Mark 10:19

G GOD

… god so loved the world…
He gave his son…

John 3:16

GOD *has the whole world in his hands.*

H HEAVEN

…our Father
who art in
HEAVEN…

Matthew 6:9

I IDOL

…an IDOL of gold and silver is not the true GOD.

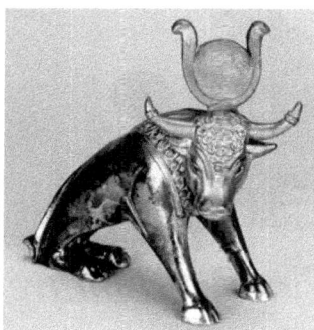

J JOHN

…There was a man sent from GOD, whose name was JOHN.

John 1:6

John baptized many

K KISS

...Greet one another with a Holy KISS.

2 Corinthians 13:12
1 Thessalonians 5:26

L LIGHT/LOVE

…Let your LIGHT shine…

Matthew 5:16

…GOD is Love.

John 4:8

M

MOTHER/MARY
…Mary, Mother of Jesus, who is called Christ.

Matthew 1:16

N NOAH'S ARK

...NOAH'S ARK was
a big boat filled
with all the
animals.

O OBEY

…Children obey your parents in the Lord, for this is right.

Ephesians 6:1

P PRAY

...PRAY at all times ...

Ephesians 6:18

Q QUICK

…be QUICK
and steadfast
in the Lord.

R REJOICE

…REJOICE in the
Lord always…
Philippians 4:4

S STUDY

...STUDY to show yourself approved ...

2 Timothy 2:15

T THOMAS/ TWELVE

…THOMAS was one of the TWELVE apostles.

U UNITY

…maintain the UNITY of the spirit…

Ephesians 4:3

V VINE

…I am the VINE…

John 15:5

Henry O. Adkins

W WORSHIP

…WORSHIP the Lord your GOD…

Matthew 4:9

X Xylophone

With GOD and a xylophone we make pretty Music…

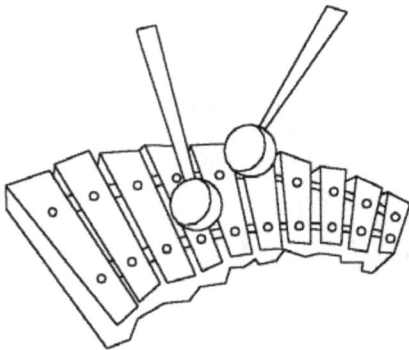

Y YOKE

…Take my YOKE upon you..

Matthew 11:29

Z ZEAL

…have ZEAL for GOD…

Romans 10:2

ABCDE

FGHIJ

KLMNO

PQRSTUV

WXYZ

1234567890

Other Cheudi Publications

Life Lessons Henry O. Adkins

Common Sense Your Way Through College
Henry O. Adkins

After The Beginning In The Garden Sue L. Adkins

Raising Great Kids Henry and Sue L. Adkins

Kwanzaa Celebration Sue L. Adkins

Out of The Corner Of My Eye Sue L. Adkins

String Town Sue L. Adkins

Henry O. Adkins

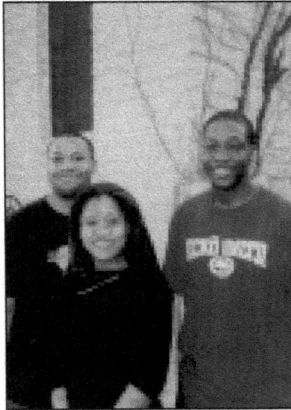

This book is dedicated to my children
Angela, Morgan and Cryston.
Thanks to my
lovely wife Sue, for giving me these three
wonderful bookworms

About The Author

Henry O. Adkins, is an Author, Inspirational Speaker, Musician, Artist, College Professor and Public Administrator, who for the last thirty years have worked with the Community in Human Services, but Henry believes that his greatest job has been a good husband and the raising of the children that God entrusted to him.

Cheudi Publishing
P.O. Box 940572
Plano, Texas 75094-0572